they are really molluscs

Anna Cathenka

Flirtation #1

salò press

Some of these poems appeared previously in the following journals: *Burning House Press, Cardiff Review, HVTN, Lighthouse, Norwich: A Dostoyevksy Wannabe Cities Anthology, Poetry: anthology for the 2017/18 MA Creative Writing at UEA by Eggbox Press, Stride, Volta: An Obscurity Of Poets*

978-1-9165021-0-9

Printed and Bound by 4Edge

Cover design and layout by Salò Press
Art by Ernst Haeckel

Typeset by Sophie Essex

Published by:
Salò Press
85 Gertrude Road
Norwich
UK

editorsalòpress@gmail.com
www.salòpress.weebly.com

for my mum

The Observer's Books were pocket guides, published by Frederick Warne & Co between 1937 and 1983. These poems are written after the following publications in the series:

- The Observer's Book of Sea and Seashore
- The Observer's Book of British Geology
- The Observer's Book of Larger British Moths

Contents

PREFACE

It is not of course possible to include the whole of the *Anna Cathenka* in a work of this size, but for a long time past it has been the desire of the poet to present to the observant public an introduction to this fascinating field of study.
It happens that the whole of the larger of our *Anna Cathenka*, including those which fly in the day-time and those having the largest and most conspicuous of
practically the whole of this important group
large divisions
has been omitted entirely.

This does not mean that they should be entirely disregarded,

illustrations are approximately life-size
(exceptions of eggs)

Since this excellent series is available for the serious student, the author of the present book has omitted details of the adult *Anna Cathenka* and relied on coloured illustrations. The descriptions of the   are short, partly to enable the book to be kept small, and brief field notes have been added.
It is hoped that the result, which can so easily be slipped into the pocket, will provide the observer with an introduction in the field to the study of this compulsive subject.

BEST OBSERVED FROM THE INTERIOR OF A SEA-CAVE

Slightly encouraged, he dipped his brush
in the sea – John Ashbery, 'The Painter'

The colour of the sea
is modified by the particles
which float in it; by
the angle from which it is
viewed; by the clearness
of the day; by reflection
from the sky; by the clouds;
by the adjacent cliffs; and,
in the shallows, by the colour
of the sea-floor. It varies

from a dull, leaden grey in gloomy
weather; or from the yellow
or brown of a muddy
river mouth to a delightful
blue or green, or off parts of the coast
of Cornwall to a milky white from
China clay workings; on a bright
Summer's day it may be the rich
purple of the Ancient
Greek's 'wine-coloured sea'.

Water has a slightly bluish
tint which intercepts the reds
of the daylight and the yellows
more quickly so that only the blues
and greens
can penetrate; a white

object in the water turns blue
before sinking. Beneath the sea
objects appear floodlit by a strong white
light but as the observer moves away they appear increasingly
blue.

SOME SEASHORE SIGHTS

you are not SOME SEASHORE SIGHTS
                    IN THE SKY
so i'll look for those instead –
sights in the heavens difficult to notice inland

(yes!)

and i will find the afterglow – false dawn – zodiacal light
none of which are you
you are also not the counterglow
which moves at night from east to west across the sky
to stay opposite the sun

(oh!)

i will go to scotland and other northerly regions
when you don't
to see the northern lights

you are not SOME SEASHORE SIGHTS
                    IN THE AIR
although conditions do make you seem
bigger and closer than you actually are
neither are you a mirage

you are not SOME SEASHORE SIGHTS
                    IN THE SEA
so i'll go to intemperate zones
where icebergs drift, constituting
a serious menace to navigation

(ah!)

you are not a water-spout
even if there is something of the tornado about you
so my eyes are fixed on the horizon

you are not SOME SEASHORE SIGHTS
                    ON SHIPS
namely st. elmo's fire (let's not

talk about electricity)
hell you are not

SOME ANCIENT LEGENDS so i
will keep watch for a kraken

CRABS

the fiddler crab is described as pugnacious

you are a fiddler crab

the long-legged spider-crab moves in a slow, undulating manner

you are a long-legged spider-crab

the pea crab is an example of parasitism

you are a pea crab

the masked crab has fanciful markings

you are a masked crab

the sea-spiders seem to be 'all legs'

you are a sea-spider

the long-haired porcelain crab is not fond of mud

you are a long-haired porcelain crab

the common hermit crab lives in an abandoned shell

you are a common hermit crab

the devil's crab is quite large

you are a devil's crab

MOTHS

I have decided to use moths in this poem as a metaphor for
my prevailing sexualities, such as:

THE HAWK MOTHS (particularly in terms of behaviour). IE:

Death's Head
Convolvulus
Spurge
Bedstraw
Small Elephant
Humming-Bird

Or in reference specifically to cunnilingus, THE
PROMINENT MOTHS (*Swallow Prominent, Lesser
Swallow Prominent, Three-Humped Prominent, Great
Prominent, Coxcomb Prominent, Scarce Prominent,* etc.)

See also: *Buff-Tip Moth, Chocolate-Tip Moth, Buff Arches
Moth.*

Can't even mention my *Glaucous Shears*, my *Broad-barred
White* teeth, the *Grey Dagger* on your *Splendid Brocade*.
Such *Pale Stigma*, my *Black Collar, Flame Shoulder* and
Great Dart. All gone *Southern Rustic* with underuse. Ah,
True Lover's Knot!

but beyond base behavioural activity, desire
like how i love men with a sort of *Kentish Glory*

want to be with women as a *Red-Necked Footman*
it is this that makes me masculine, my *Light Crimson
Underwing*

i am a *Ghost Swift* in the night, cackling with the camp

Fox Moths, the *Drinker Moths* – vada that *Lackey Moth*,
girls

but with a *Satin Lutestring*. always a but

like *Scarce Silver Lines* like

but i will become an *Old Lady Moth*, no *Figure of Eighty* for
December Moth

o me

i would take my sexualities then and retire to the woods
become *Oak Egger*, *Grass Egger*, *Pale Oak Egger*, and
eventually

Small Egger, crawl underleaf and remember

Dark Tussock Moth
Puss Moth
Ruby Tiger Moth

TERRIBLE LIZARD

although actually there's no
reason to imbue a poem
about dinosaurs
with metaphor –

frequent line breaks
will do, the occasional
linguistic invocation
such as *cretaceous*

or *ichthyosaur*
thrown in for good measure
creates the effect *stumpy legs*
of this being a poem

about dinosaurs
brontosaurus and everything
that suggests –
extinction, obsolescence

etc. no need
to be heavy handed
diPLODocus. diPLODocus.
or sure

footed. tsk. this is
a poem about dinosaurs
clever girl, just call it
terrible lizard

after all
there are not many
poems about dinosaurs
triceratops so just

the thought is enough:
line break
line break
stegosaurus

what's the magic
word?
jurassic (ripples)
    ((in the water))

BOOM!
BOOM!
BOOM!
spinal plates

Hwæt –
this is a poem
about dinosaurs
tiny brains

SOLID ROCK

strange as it may seem
several types of animal
bore tunnels into solid rock

all most of us will see of them
are the holes
they leave behind. i just knew

that if i could find something in
THE OBSERVER'S BOOK OF SEA AND SEASHORE
about movement

i could write about you –
is there such thing
as a sea-wolf?

i thought there might be
reference to some maned
urchin or pelagic dancer

that moves gracefully
through the water
that steals upon its prey

soundlessly before
hypnotising them into submission
some golden mollusc

or lionized starfish, a stealthy
swagger-crab to say
there's something about

the way you move
but, just like you, there's
no obvious metaphor

except, of course, the earth itself
which compared with the restless
ever-moving sea

appears to be changeless
and immoveable
THE OBSERVER'S BOOK OF SEA AND SEASHORE

goes on accordingly to note
how this, however,
is an illusion.

THAT POEM[1] BY BERNSTEIN has put me
in
       a

ba–
             d
                   mood

though I couldn't say why. the chief food is beech leaves
  and they
are not easy to obtain
even in beech woods. i am writing
this poem with the washing machine
on. it is my meter. it is as loud as
Henry VIII. there are other trees
on which it will feed
but they are not the place to search, they are dark
rather shiny brown
with the last segment blown out
and held cocked
over the back. it looks
most uninviting to pick up. i guess this
is the rinse cycle. or S –
       P
             I
N?
amirite charles? the lobster
moth is restricted, but later

DEVELOP INTO GROTESQUE INSECTS

the head of the larva is thrown back when alarmed
and the legs are then spread out
and if Anne Boleyn were a tumble dryer she still wouldn't
be a loud

[1] 'Me and My Pharoah', Charles Bernstein, Poetry, Volume 204, April 2014, pp. 51-60

THE FOOD OF MOTH LARVA

sallow and willow / apple trees / poplar / potato leaves / Duke of Argyll's tea rose / honeysuckle, sweet tobacco plants and petunias / privet, lilac and ash / pine needles / bedstraw / grapevine, fuchsias, dock and antirrhinum / greater willow-herb or fireweed / flowers of bugle / flowers of valerian / birch and alder / beech, oak and other trees / aspen, black poplar / hazel / maple / lime / bramble and low-growing bushes / raspberry canes / broom or heather / elm and also cultivated fruit trees and hops / garden roses / hawthorn, blackthorn and sea-buckthorn / various conifers / plum / viburnum, dogwood, ivy and ling / grasses, kidney-vetch / bilberry / the crisp leaves of reeds / the small-leaved lime / osier / practically any low-growing plant / water-dock, water-mint, yellow loosestrife and a few other marsh plants / elder / dandelion leaves / plantains / common rock-rose and salad burnet / nettle / white dead-nettle / groundsel / comfrey / sheep's fescue grass / forget-me-not and borage / ragwort / lichens / firs / the roots of grass / decaying wood / sycamore trees

(THEY ARE REALLY MOLLUSCS)

maybe they could be brittle-stars
they'd like that, having
something of the delicate

galaxy about them, all compact bodies
and slender arms but perhaps
they are actually sea-urchins, some

dickensian mermaids, heart-shaped.
she could be, say, the purple heart
urchin and she could be the common

heart urchin. they aren't
sea-lilies because they only have four
arms to wave about in the water

so maybe a stunted star-fish?
sometimes in bed there is
something of the limpet

about at least one of them
they are both
cute little periwinkles

dressed in necklace-shells
and cowries, silly whelks. they could
easily be nudibranches (misspelt)

because in spite of their forbidding
name and the absence
of a shell the sea-slugs (nudibranchs)

include some of the most
beautiful seashore animals.
one day they are sea-slaters,

sandhoppers, etc – one is
an aesop prawn (fabled)
and the other

a chameleon shrimp (fickle)
they eat picnics as blennies
and butterfish, joke *coal-fish*

flat-fish, one angrily calls the other
a stickleback
(says sorry later, the sucker-fish)

she finds out weever is a sting-fish
and they are sea-scorpions with stings
in their tails before they finally

become sea-birds
knots, terns, waders
and discover

there are also small shore-beetles
living under stones or in
rock crevices

SEAMIST

can we be the seamist?

neither the water nor the air?

done by lunch?

can we be the between

thing that barely touches

land except on very dark days

when we're nearly rain?

can we draw a line   please that is not quite   one thing

or the other

having the potential to become

heavenly clouds

or just separate into single states

no drama? i'd like to be

the cool dawn air

you can be deep

and colder like the water

by which I mean, rise up into me

THE CAVITY BEARER

if i were a sponge
i'd have no spongin
nor limy or flinty spicules
like a slime sponge

i'd be a boring sponge
able to excavate holes
in shells and do much damage
to oyster beds if i were a sponge

i'd give no sign of life either
other than making small
currents in the water
around me if i were a sponge

i'd be strengthened
by horny material
i might be colourful
and my size and shape

vary with the conditions
in which i lived if i were a
sponge i'd also seem so
inert as to be mistaken

for a plant
and simply consist
of a soft spongy substance
if i were a sponge

A PIOUS FRAUD

enstoned you have become

a headless snake, fossilized

miraculously by hilda

a yorkshire saint.

o you cretaceous ammonite!

o you rotten flint!

you have become everything

I feared, your stone heart

a shepherd's mitre. you have formed

a difference in the shallow

london waters. return to your bed

trilobite, relic, dense belemnite –

carve yourself your own

fraudulent head. a plague on you,

dead mollusc, of a thousand

dudley locusts!

EL MAR

after Jorge Luis Borges

The waves also
grind the pebbles and sand
against the sea-floor, smoothing
its irregularities and slowly
wearing it away.

¿Quién es el mar? The sea
attacks not merely the face
of the cliffs but the debris piled up
at their feet. The larger fragments,
too heavy to move, meet the brunt
of the sea's attack and for a time
protect the land from further destruction.

In doing so they themselves are destroyed.
¿Quién soy? The waves,
which consist of tons of water hurled
violently and almost incessantly
against the shore,
do far more than level the sand
and discolour the rocks.

¿Quién es aquel violento? They tear across
beaches and leap against the sea-walls
and the piers; they have wrenched
apart the massive blocks
of an esplanade, tons in weight and clamped
together. They drive the air before them
and compress it against the cliff face.
El mar, el siempre mar. Thus the waves

destroy the cliffs, undermining them
until their upper part
collapses.

Publication details and special thanks:

Anna would like to thank the editors of the magazines, websites and anthologies where many of these poems first appeared. '(They Are Really Molluscs)' was originally published in *HVTN*; 'Some Seashore Sights' and 'Terrible Lizard' were originally published in the Dostoyevsky Wannabe Cities anthology *Norwich*; 'That Poem by Bernstein' was originally published in *Stride*; 'Crabs' was originally published in *Eyeflash*; 'Moths' was originally published in the Salò Press Volta reading series anthology *An Obscurity of Poets*; 'Seamist' was originally published in *Lighthouse* journal; 'The Food of Moth Larva' was originally published by *Burning House Press*; 'Best Observed from the Interior of a Sea-Cave' was published by *Cardiff Review*; 'Preface' was originally published in the *Poetry* anthology for the 2017/18 MA Creative Writing at UEA by Eggbox Press.

Anna would like to personally thank the following people for their support in the production of this chapbook: Tiffany Atkinson; Kate Birch and the team at *Ink, Sweat and Tears*; Sophie Essex; the Falmouth Seven Stars Poets; Susan Kruse and Philip Goundrey; Sophie Robinson; Emily and John Stewart Rayner; and the UEA 2017/18 MA Poetry cohort.